Colonel A. J. D. Biddle's

New Illustrated

DO OR DIE

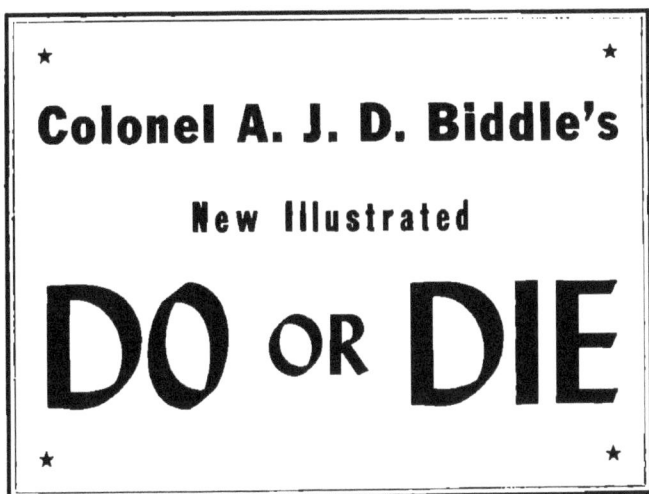

The Naval & Military Press Ltd

Published by

The Naval & Military Press Ltd
Unit 5 Riverside, Brambleside
Bellbrook Industrial Estate
Uckfield, East Sussex
TN22 1QQ England

Tel: +44 (0)1825 749494

www.naval-military-press.com
www.nmarchive.com

Introduction to New Edition

THIS war has proven the value of training our Marines in the art of hand-to-hand combat, weaponless defense and proficiency with the bayonet. In helping with this phase of our training, Colonel A. J. Drexel Biddle has contributed greatly. Not only has his manual "Do or Die" been a basic text, it has also been the text book of a new kind of bayonet fighting. The flat bayonet style with his "parry, right step, hand cut, slash" movements is being taught to Marines everywhere.

In this new edition, the basic text remains the same except for the changes necessitated in the use of the slash over the point system of fighting. We have attempted through more photographs to better show these movements.

The author now directs, in his extensive individual teaching of the bayonet and knife, to slash at the throat instead of thrusting with the point. The slash is most effective used left to right, directly following the left parry, right step and hand cut.

It is important that we point out at this time that in combat, if your rifle is loaded, shoot a man rather than engage him in a bayonet fight. Unless you are under orders for a bayonet charge, the bullet is quicker and more accurate than the bayonet. However, the bayonet is an effective and dangerous weapon when used correctly by a well-trained Marine. Every Marine should become proficient in its use.

THE PUBLISHERS.

Foreword

THERE is greater need of training the individual soldier than ever before. The tendency in modern warfare to utilize cover and to spread out more and more in the attack, in order to escape the devastating fire of the defender has forced the infantryman to rely primarily on his own personal skill, agility and courage to get forward and close with the enemy. The old linear and mass attacks have been replaced by small groups of skirmishers, working forward with calculated boldness and stealth, seeking out the defender's weak spots, in order to assault his combat groups. New methods of attack will require that the infantryman be a skirmisher, marksman, athlete and fighter par excellence.

The fighting powers of the individual soldier have increased in importance while mere weight of numbers has lost much of its value on the fireswept battlefield of today. Not only must the infantryman create his own opportunities, but he must be imbued more than ever with an aggressive spirit and a confidence in his own superiority, because he must depend on his own resourcefulness in battle.

Whether or not we believe the bayonet is still worth retaining as a weapon, bayonet fighting or its refinement, bayonet fencing, as illustrated in this manual, remains a part and parcel of the individual's training as heretofore. No other form of training instills greater confidence in the prowess of the soldier or creates that self-determination and overwhelming impulse to close with the enemy than is fostered by bayonet training. Herein lies its great value.

Self-preservation remains the great law of Nature. It is the heritage of every soldier to know how to protect himself under all situations. The assault will often lead to personal contact with the enemy, when the individual must know how to destroy his opponent and at the same time protect himself.

Individual combat, whether it be in the form of boxing, knife fighting, hand-to-hand encounter, or the Greco-Roman catch-as-catch-can and Jiu-Jitsu wrestling, develops a suppleness of body, an agility afoot, a quickness of eye and a coördination of mind and body that adds immeasurably to the self-reliance and courage of the soldier in the close-up encounter with the enemy.

Colonel A. J. D. Biddle, USMCR, with his extraordinary background of experience and study, has contributed in this text a most valuable and practical analysis of individual combat for developing the soldier's fighting and physical attributes. This manual combines the art of self-defense and illustrates the methods of attack that will enhance the individual's natural powers of destruction.

C. J. MILLER,
Colonel, U. S. Marines.

Imprimatur

THE writer has been an ardent student of the art of self-defense in all of its branches. During the past twenty-five years he has pursued an intensive study and training in the use of fencing blades. In the course of these studies he has sought every opportunity to obtain instruction and personal training under the most eminent authorities and experts in the United States and abroad. It is with the knowledge and experience so gained that he now undertakes the preparation of this manual.

Grateful recognition is accorded to all who have contributed to his knowledge or collaborated in the preparation of this work. Special mention must be made of some whose contributions are of outstanding value.

The writer has been trained by able sword and bayonet instructors of the British Army, including Sergeant J. H. Dawkins, the sword instructor of the King's Royal Horse Guards in London; he has received special instruction in bayonet combat at the military training school of Gondrecourt, in France, and in sword and dagger in several Portuguese, Spanish and French Colonies.

Lessons in broadsword were received from the broadsword champion, M. Thomas, at the Cercle Hoche in Paris where the writer also received instructions in general swordsmanship from the famous former international sword champion, M. Surget, also an instructor at the Cercle. Afterwards the writer pursued

5

his fencing studies under the celebrated fencing master, Mr. J. Martinez Castello in New York.

Many years ago the writer began his instructions under the teachings of a former American fencing champion who, a few years since, won the bayonet fighting championship of the world. This latter named gentleman is Major William J. Herrmann, PMTC, to whom the writer is thankful for the knowledge of some of the bayonet and knife movements prescribed in this treatise. Major Herrmann conducts the famous William J. Herrmann Physical Culture Institute in Philadelphia where special attention is given by the major and his fine staff to the instruction of teachers in bayonet, knife, and sword fencing.

In 1935 the Fifth Regiment of Marines commanded by Major General (then Colonel) Charles F. B. Price, USMC, was stationed at Marine Barracks, Quantico, Virginia, as part of the Fleet Marine Force, under command of Major General Charles H. Lyman, now retired.

The enthusiastic interest of the first and subsequent regimental commanders of the Fifth Regiment in training for individual combat brought about an invitation to the writer to come to Quantico personally to serve as instructor to the Fifth Marines; it was his privilege to do this in August and September of 1935.

The gratifying results attained during that period of training created the desirability of developing this type of training further, and General Price suggested to the writer the preparation of this manual to be used as a guide in future instruction.

The writer is particularly grateful to the general for that suggestion and for the encouragement and coöperation since ex-

6

tended by valuable suggestions and by personally directing the preparation of illustrations.

As this manual would not have come into being save for General Price's timely suggestions and valuable assistance, and because the general is an outstanding commander and an enthusiastic advocate of training in individual combat in the Marine Corps, it is a special pleasure to be allowed to dedicate this manual to:

MAJOR GENERAL CHARLES F. B. PRICE
United States Marines.

Changes of command following the maneuvers with the Fleet in 1935 took Major General Lyman to command of the Marine Barracks, Quantico, brought Colonel (now Brigadier General, retired) James J. Meade to command of the First Marine Brigade, Fleet Marine Force, took the then Colonel Price to executive of that brigade and brought Colonel Harold L. Parsons to command of the Fifth Marines. The writer tenders heartfelt thanks to these officers; the interest and encouragement they gave during the entire period of the writer's service as instructor to the Fifth Marines have proven most helpful in the writer's completion of his undertaking.

During the period of his service as instructor, the writer enjoyed the able assistance of Lieutenant Colonels James M.

7

Masters, Sr., USMC, and William A. Kengla, USMC (then both lieutenants). These two latter named gentlemen were formerly pupils of the writer in individual combat at the United States Marine Corps Basic School for Officers: they are both fine swordsmen. Being of inventive genius, Colonels Masters and Kengla devised several excellent new forms of attack and defense, as shown in this treatise.

Now come the very latest developments in the art of Defendu (originated by the celebrated Mr. W. E. Fairbairn, assistant commissioner, Shanghai Municipal Police), and of Jiu-Jitsu as shown by Lieut. Col. Samuel G. Taxis, USMC, formerly stationed at Shanghai: there, in addition to his other military duties, he was instructor in these arts. Following a series of conferences with Colonel Taxis several of his particularly noteworthy assaults are described in Part III of this manual. Mr. Fairbairn is author of the book, "Get Tough."

As instructor for the Bureau of Investigation, the U. S. Department of Justice, the writer instructs in individual combat under command of J. Edgar Hoover.

The writer owes an especial debt of gratitude to the world-famous all-around athlete, the late Colonel C. J. Miller, former commander of the Fifth Regiment of Marines. Under Colonel Miller's personal instruction, the war regiments were trained and developed in athletic prowess. The colonel personally engaged in contests of strength and skill against the "pick of the men." As an American bayonet fighting champion and as one of the boxing instructors of the Marine Corps, he discovered and trained several champions. The greatest of those whose training he encouraged proved to be the only perpetually undefeated retired heavyweight world's champion in the history of the ring, the mighty Marine, Gene Tunney, now in the Navy

8

but until recently captain in the Marine Corps Reserve. The friendship of Colonel Miller was an ever brilliant source of inspiration to the writer.

In the summer of 1936 the writer was signally honored by again serving as combat instructor under the distinguished command of Colonel Miller, who had succeeded to the command of the Fifth Regiment, United States Marine Corps.

During his terms of service as combat instructor on the staff of the faculty of the Marine Corps Base School for Student Officers the writer has had the privilege and advantage of serving, as combat instructor, under the successive brilliant commands of Major General (then Colonel) Philip M. Torrey, Colonel (now retired) A. D. Rorex, Colonel (now retired) William Dulty Smith, Major General (then Colonel) Julian C. Smith and Major General (then Colonel) A. H. Turnage. Owing to the gracious personal interest taken by each of these particularly able officers, the writer was at all times accorded every advantage enabling him to develop and improve his work. He received infinite inspiration and continual encouragement from the Commanding Officer at Headquarters of the Marine Corps Schools, the late distinguished Lieutenant (then Major) General J. C. Breckinridge.

The writer has served in the United States Marine Corps as combat instructor during consecutive terms of office of the following Commandants: Major General George Barnett, Major General John A. Lejeune, Major General Ben H. Fuller, Major General John H. Russell, and General Thomas Holcomb, and now he has the continued honor to serve under the present Commandant of the United States Marine Corps, Lieut. General Alexander Vandegrift.

A. J. D. B.

Col. A. J. D. Biddle, right, Master of the Bayonet, with a pupil.

Master of the Bayonet

BY ROBERT H. MYERS

A most unusual man is Colonel A. J. Drexel Biddle, US-MCR. He is noted for being kind, thoughtful, generous and gracious. He is also noted for his ability to snap a man's neck, break an opponent's arm or otherwise render him painfully useless in a matter of split seconds.

Thousands of United States Marines, old and new in the service, have met the colorful colonel. Many more will have the good fortune to meet him and see him in action as the months roll on. They will find him kindly, helpful and understanding.

And ten minutes later they may find themselves flat on their backs with the colonel's knee jammed in their stomachs.

"Now here's another hold," Colonel Biddle will say, permitting the pupil to get to his feet. "Straighten your hand like this." He will stiffen his hand into what he calls "the Japanese fist." "Now bring it down like this . . ." The colonel's hand will be brought down in a sharp, blade-like manner on the student's collar bone. "You can break a man's collar bone with that one blow," the colonel will explain.

The student will have no difficulty understanding the feat, nor will he doubt its effectiveness. Colonel Biddle leaves no room for doubt. That's why he is recognized as one of the greatest experts in the world in the art of hand-to-hand combat, a science to which he has devoted, not the leisure hours of a hobby, but the full years of a busy, productive life. Today this man with the broad heavy shoulders and firm jaw executes every

11

movement of his art with confidence, accuracy and incredible speed. He has learned thoroughly how to use the tools of his trade, the tools being the naked bayonet, the knife and his two bare hands.

The career of Colonel Biddle, novel and varied, excites the imagination and challenges the adjective. Rich man, sportsman, society figure, teacher, preacher, boxer, publisher, adventurer; a man who tore down convention and built a reputation—that has been the life of Colonel Biddle for lo, these many years. He kept a box at the opera and a ringside seat at the fights; he shook hands with the intellectuals one night, and traded jabs with pugilists the next. Debutantes of the upper crust and the "dese and dose" guys of the streets knew him affectionately as "Tony" Biddle, and Tony Biddle could lead a cotillon or with his left with equal efficiency. He had the happy knack of keeping one foot firmly on the social ladder and the other in the sports ring.

You have heard of the Cabots and the Lodges of Back Bay Boston who spoke to no one except the Cabots and the Lodges and God. Well, the Biddles — the Main Line Biddles of old Philadelphia—had the same distinction, but Tony Biddle doesn't operate that way. He speaks to everyone, and everyone loves it.

Physical and spiritual development soon became Colonel Biddle's mission in life. That was why he declined to remain on the retired roll when World War II came along; that is why today he carries on a vigorous day-in and day-out schedule that would exhaust the energy and enthusiasm of a man much younger than himself. Teaching the secrets of his knowledge to young Americans in general and Marines in particular is Colonel Biddle's life.

He showed me a lot of holds and movements, his enthusiasm

mounting. There was the strangle hold and the way it can be broken. After you break it you indulge in a little play of your own, such as gouging out your opponent's eyes or jamming his nose in the general direction of his forehead.

"Dirty fighting?" He laughed. "Call it that if you want to, but the dirtiest fighting in the world is Jiu-Jitsu." This struck a significant chord. "Dirty fighting" is usually associated with gouging, kicking a foe in the groin, yanking off an ear. Some pantywaists abhor "dirty fighting," even in a war against admittedly dirty fighters such as the Japs and Nazis. But Jiu-Jitsu, they reason, not knowing a thing about it, is a clean, honorable combat science. Colonel Biddle agrees that it is a highly developed science, but it isn't clean.

I looked at his two index fingers. The left one was bent, but the right one looked like nothing except a cork-screw. "Clean, scientific" Japs were responsible for the breaks.

Colonel Biddle held the right one out and told its story.

"I got that in a match with a Jap. We were using rifles and bayonets.

"I disarmed him and his rifle fell on the ground. Quick as a flash he had the finger, gave it a twist and broke it." Biddle wrestled his opponent to the ground but the Jap judges called the match a draw.

Jiu-Jitsu, he explained, is 4,000 years old, and the Japs have carried it on as a national pastime. Universities are operated to teach the science exclusively, and young Nips get the fundamentals at about the same time they get a diaper.

But Colonel Biddle is very positive about one point: the Japs are not as good as newly taught Yanks in the art. For one thing, he declared, the Jap simply doesn't think as fast as we do. "That's been proven time and again on the battlefield and in the air," he observed, adding that fast thinking is imperative in hand-to-hand combat such as this.

Then he told another story which was a distinct surprise. Contrary to general belief, Jiu-Jitsu was a dead sport or science in Japan for several hundred years until, of all people, an Irish-American named O'Brien revived it some 40 or 50 years ago. O'Brien was a seafaring man who ran across the science when he met an old Samurai warrior in Nagasaki. The Japs, whose ancestors had reveled in the sport, readopted it.

O'Brien became quite a figure in Nagasaki, but later came back to this country. Colonel Biddle met him in Philadelphia and promptly engaged him as an instructor in the mid-twenties. He studied under O'Brien for a year and a half, and with his previously mastered training in the foil, bayonet, boxing and knife fighting, soon became a master of Jiu-Jitsu. Mrs. Biddle, incidentally, studied for six months and knows some fine points of the sport herself.

"American boys take to this stuff like ducks to water. They love it." The colonel beamed as he said this. He beams every time mention is made of these things.

Anecdotes and information well from the colonel. His love of contact sports dates back to the years when he won numerous amateur boxing titles, fighting as a heavyweight. He was a personal friend of Bob Fitzsimmons.

"What a master of science he was." He paused to remove a wrist watch, a present from Gene Tunney at the time this ex-Marine was training for the first Dempsey fight. "I'll show you the famed solar-plexus punch Fitzsimmons used."

Perhaps you'd like to try it on, say, a Jap. Here's how it was worked, and Colonel Biddle should know. He boxed with Ruby Robert enough times to learn it. He showed it to me, but

14

luckily he pulled his punches. He throws a right that is almost a hook. If it lands, well and good. If it doesn't—follow on through, your right foot stepping forward and somewhat behind your opponent's left leg, virtually pinning it momentarily. Your left hand, meanwhile, held close to the body, is well down, almost to the floor. Come up quickly, your right elbow barely missing your opponent's face and your left—a terrific punch following the momentum of the shoulder movement—lands in the solar plexus. This ought to drop your opponent dead as a sack of cement, but if you lower your left and come up again quickly, you can smash him on the point of the jaw as his body falls toward you.

"This drives the jaw bones into the brain and you can kill a man," the colonel explained lightly.

It was Gene Tunney, incidentally, who once declared, "Colonel Biddle would have been a world champion if he had gone into the game as a professional." The colonel, returning the compliment, termed Tunney "the best boxing fighter in the history of the ring."

The colonel should know. He boxed with the best in the world over a period of 51 years before retiring from public appearances at the age of 60. His most notable appearances were

against Fitzsimmons, Philadelphia Jack O'Brien, rugged Peter Maher, Jack Johnson, Kid McCoy, Lightweight Champion Frank Erne and Georges Carpentier.

Interesting it is that the Frenchman, Carpentier, made but three public appearances in the ring in this country. One was against Jack Dempsey, another against Gene Tunney and the third, prior to the others, was against Biddle. Many years later Champion Tunney told Biddle that it was as he watched his match with Carpentier that he planned his own fighting campaign if he should ever subsequently meet Carpentier in the ring.

Of his match with the clever Johnson, Colonel Biddle remarked, "That was a tough bout. It took me a week to get over it."

The colonel named James J. Corbett as the greatest boxer in the game, Fitzsimmons the greatest fighter, and Tunney the greatest boxing-fighter. You can see the distinctions.

Of course, one of the smartest men was Philadelphia Jack O'Brien, an intimate friend of Colonel Biddle. They boxed in public exhibitions more than 100 times, and attracted a sell-out crowd one time in Cincinnati. Colonel Biddle was a sparring partner for O'Brien for all his professional matches, and O'Brien helped him train over a 35-year period for his amateur engagements.

The colonel became interested in active sports long before he became an intimate of the great names of sport—famous figures dating from the turn of the century on down through the Golden Era of the '20's. It seems that at the age of 10 he had to learn knife fighting.

"We lived on the Portuguese island of Madeira and knife fighting was a popular pastime, such as boxing is to boys in

16

this country. By gum, we had some fights in those days." One of the colonel's strongest phrases is "By gum!"

It was only natural that years later he became proficient in other types of knife work; types known as the Spanish Knife and the Bowie Knife. He considers the latter, and teaches it to Marines, the highest form of knife fighting. He even went west, at the suggestion of his friend, the late Colonel C. J. Miller, USMC, to study the technique of stoccata, in-quartata and passato sotto with the Bowie Knife.

The career of Colonel Biddle embraces so many phases and stretches over so many years it is difficult to correlate them. Nor did we try to during the day I spent with him. People and incidents crowd the years. For instance, he showed me a sunken place in his chest. He got it "sparring" with a 245-pound friend during a bout in the garage of the Biddle mansion. (He "neglected" to see a physician about the broken ribs, which caused the sunken condition.)

Knife wounds? Plenty of them. Bayonet wounds? Well, two years ago an FBI agent got to him with a bayonet. "It just missed my intestines by one-seventeenth of an inch, if you can imagine that distance.

"What was worse, though—it was a rusty blade." The colonel laughed. They figured the wound would put him on the sidelines for six or seven weeks. "I was up and around in a week." Thereafter, however, it was suggested that Colonel Biddle wear a mask and protector when instructing pupils.

He figures he has schooled within the past several years, some 150,000 men in combat work. Most of them worked with bare blades; the colonel with a scabbarded blade. It's a wonder he doesn't have more bayonet and knife scars.

He has his selections for the best bayonet, Jiu-Jitsu and Judo

17

men he has trained. He named them as Lieutenant Colonel Alan Shapley, Captain Stephen Stavers, Captain Edward L. Katzenbach, Jr., Sergeant Tommy Loughran, the retired undefeated light-heavyweight boxing champion, Sergeants C. E. Zimmer, Thierbach, Quigley, and First Sergeant Bill Crystal.

How does Colonel Biddle keep up the pace? Enthusiasm! Eight years ago his doctor told him he would have to give up this strenuous schedule, or at least cut down on it. Biddle disagreed strongly.

"I love this work. I have made it my life's work. It is recreation for me. It is my life. I told him I wouldn't want to live another day if I couldn't continue."

So the doctor placed the colonel on a strict vegetable diet. "I cannot have any fattening vegetables, such as potatoes, and I haven't had a drink of liquor in eight years." He smiled and commented, "I never was a heavy drinker. I didn't get drunk. But I took a drink whenever I wanted it." Today his only vice is cigar smoking. He keeps one going most of the day. "Funny that they don't seem to hurt me, isn't it?" he asked.

Do the Marines get "Black Death" schooling? Yes. Plenty of it. And it might be added that his beloved Marines can get anything Colonel Biddle has, including his life, if they want it. He is profoundly proud to be a Marine. He drums into every listener the greatness of the Corps. His activities are multiple, and when the Marines aren't calling, he is and has been for many years individual combat instructor at the schools of J. Edgar Hoover's G-Men, teaching them his art; he does the same for the National Police, whose members undergo three-month training periods under FBI sponsorship at Washington. Major General Hoyle had him train his entire Ninth Army Division in Individual Combat and concluded with a parade of the Divi-

sion in his honor. He has for years taught the police of Philadelphia. To all groups he invariably makes such observations
as, "The Marines have perfected this method. . . ." It would
be hard to beat the old boy for loyalty and pride in the Corps.
He even took time off to tell a waiter in Washington's Carlton
Hotel dining room how fine the food was with the Marines up
on the front line trenches in World War I. He wasn't critical
of anything—he merely saw an opportunity to sound off about
his beloved outfit.

His trophy room at home must be filled with cups and medals
won in his many fields of activity, and his memory book must
be overflowing with honors bestowed upon him in this country
and in Europe.

His proudest possession, however, is a letter. "It is the greatest honor I have ever received," he said. "You may read it."

"Beginning with the first World War and continuing almost
unbrokenly to the present time, you have contributed in an outstanding degree to the training of Marine Corps personnel in
hand-to-hand combat. This was made possible, first through the
perfection in that art which you yourself attained through years
of constant study and application; second, an unusual ability to
impart to others the benefit of your expert knowledge and experience; and third, a most generous giving of your time and
energies, without expense to the government, and without regard
to the personal sacrifices and the long hours of intensive physical exertion involved.

"Even since your transfer to the Honorary Retired List in
1938, on reaching the statutory retiring age of 64 years, you
have performed active duty for extended periods, at your own
request and without pay or allowances, as combat instructor to
officers and men of the Marine Corps, also without remunera-

tion to you. The efficiency of your training and instruction has, I feel, been a definite contribution to the brilliant record of the Corps during the present war.

"It is a pleasure to commend you for this exceptionally meritorious service, and to place on record the department's recognition of its unusual character and effectiveness. A copy of this letter will be made a part of your official record."

The letter is signed by Secretary of the Navy Frank Knox.

Part I
BAYONET FENCING

Fig. 1. Rifle stock should not be used to make the parry.

B AYONET fencing is a refinement in the use of the bayonet, more scientific and effective than bayonet fighting. The bayonet fencer does not look upon his piece as a combination pike and mace, but as a "blade" of which the bayonet is the point. For this reason the bayonet fencer carefully guards his rifle against possible injury; he rarely uses his butt, relying habitually on his skill with the point. There are only four butt strokes that should ever be used: one is from the "Square Guard" position and another is the *up* stroke at the groin, directly following "Left parry" as in the following command, "Left parry, butt strike, cut down, pass by." The "cross-counter" "kick" of the rifle heel at the jaw is made by a straight arm blow; so is the butt stroke at the chest *directly* delivered with the heel of the piece. None of these four butt strokes imperil the rifle's good condition. The rifle *head guard against clubbed rifle is eschewed.* Such a guard tends to reduce one's rifle to kindling wood as it is the assault of the clubbed rifle which is swung from the barrel, the stock thus becoming the striking weapon. The bayonet fencer should meet such an attack by slashing at the opponent's throat. Thus it will be seen that the bayonet fencer is more definitely instructed in marksmanship than the bayonet fighter. The bayonet fencer is instructed to keep his rifle clean and in perfect condition for shooting at all times. He should come through a bayonet charge with blood on the blade but with the rifle unsullied and unharmed. *He should parry with his bayonet, and not with his rifle* (Figure 1), and slash his *point* into his opponent as the counter against a *swinging* or clubbed rifle attack.

23

The "On Guard" Position of the Bayonet Fencer

While the stance of the bayonet fencer in the "on guard" position is similar to that prescribed in the ordinary bayonet course, there is one distinct difference. The bayonet fighting position is rigid, but absolute elasticity must be had in the fencer's "on guard" position. Figures 3 and 4 show correct positions herein prescribed. The bayonet point must be presented to the opponent with the blade flat and the edge directly to the right (as blades of every type are scientifically presented towards an opponent). Pursuant to the fencing blade position, the butt of the rifle rests laterally against the holder's crooked under-elbow and forearm. A blade attack from this lateral position is much more difficult and almost impossible to parry; it is the more powerful thrust. Furthermore, if the blade enters flatly between the ribs it can be readily withdrawn, whereas, if it is driven into the body perpendicularly it is apt to become caught or wedged between the ribs and be difficult to withdraw. Close attention is urged to the students studying Figures 3 and 4 to learn the necessary ease and grace of the bayonet *fencer's* position. If, perchance, the extended left hand or arm is wounded and it is incapacitated, the rifle's position is still maintained by its secure hold of the supporting right forearm and grasped right hand. The left foot is advanced about sixteen inches in front of the right foot. As in sword fencing or boxing the feet must not be too far apart to impede rapid movement in fencing, shifting front, or rear pacing, or side stepping.

Fig. 3. Position of
on guard: bayonet
blade turned flat.

Figure 10, representing the "at the throat" defense, also shows the attacker using the old style bayonet fighting position, with the blade edge pointed down. In all other pictures in this book, the new position is used in the attack. It will be noted that all blades with a cutting edge as recommended in the pictured guard positions of the knife and bayonet are held with the flat side up and the cutting edge directly to the right. This guard position of the bayonet directly follows the stance of the French guard position of the broadsword, excepting that in the latter "on guard" stance the right foot is advanced and the left foot is rear, while the sword is correctly held in the right hand and with edge to the right. This position of the blade insures free withdrawal of the blade if it has been deeply thrust through the ribs and into the opponent's body. The writer stresses these instructions by return to the subject of the bayonet fencer's "on guard" position (Figures 3 and 4). In any event, the throat is recommended as the ultimate target, although *feints* are more effectively executed to the body. Danger of entangling one's bayonet in the clothing of an adversary renders the thrust into the throat advisable, particularly because the throat is uncovered and the thrust there instantly fatal. The first two inches of the blade thrust is sufficient. *Through* thrusts, even at the body or any part of the anatomy, should be forbidden by the instructor. There should never be more than three inches of the blade thrust into the body, or two inches into the throat, to insure instant withdrawal.

Fig. 4. Low crouch is a variation for on guard position.

The "Square Guard" Position

Command: *"Square Guard"!*

This is best taken from *"On Guard"* position; forward foot steps back, on line with stationary rear foot, to a straddle stance, and rifle is simultaneously carried, with "On Guard" grips maintained, to horizontal position four inches below chin, barrel down. This should clear space in a crowd.

Point and Butt from Square Guard

Commands: *"Point and butt"! "Butt and point"! "To the left, point and butt"! "To the right, butt and point"! "To the rear, butt and point"! or "To the rear, point and butt."* In the latter two commands, the turning direction is designated by the first named assault, butt or point. A short step-in or a short jump-in should be executed with each of the foregoing commands.

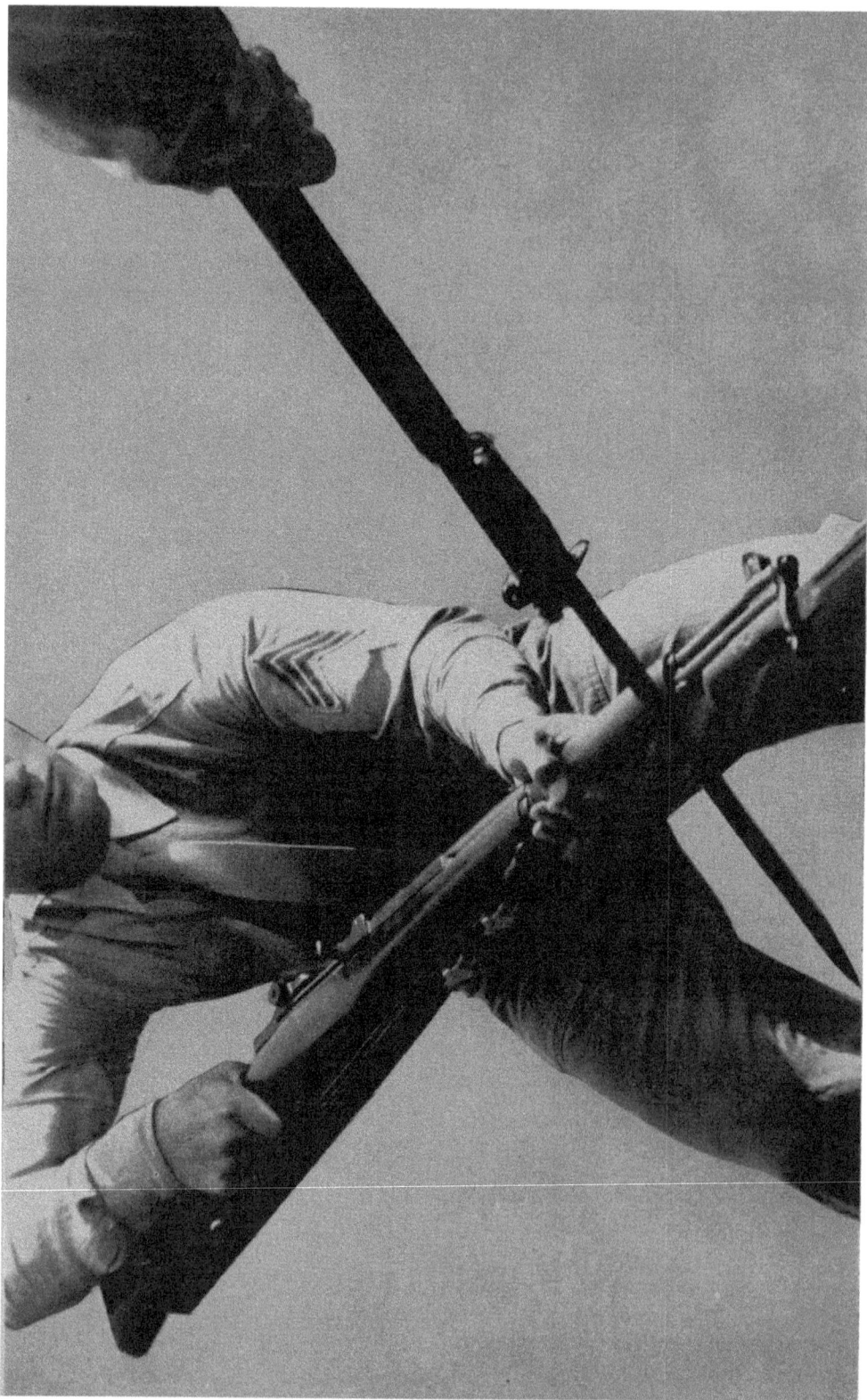

"Left Guard"

At this command, from the customary *"On Guard"* position, the left foot steps sixteen inches behind the right foot as the rifle is quickly thrown to the *left* side; grasp of right hand at balance and left hand on small of stock. Thus the *left* guard position, although opposite, resembles the stance of the customary *"On Guard"* position to the right, and the left forward hand is relieved from being further hand-cut.

Command: *"Left Parry—Butt Strike—Cut Down—Pass By"!* This movement is especially prescribed for an advancing wave in a bayonet attack at close quarters.

Each particular movement is more violently made with a *step-in* or a leaping shift of the feet. Example: The left parry is executed from the *"On Guard"* position, with the body stationary. The *"Butt Strike,"* immediately following, is made directly at the groin and is a short, direct uppercut of the butt. This is better executed by a right *step-in* or a leaping shift of the feet. *"Cut Down"!* directly follows with a left foot *step-in*, or—better still—another leaping foot shift. In practice, the three sets of movements can be consecutively taken: namely, the first set of movements with the feet stationary; second set, with a *step-in* with each consecutive movement; the third set of movements, which are the best, are each taken with a leaping shift of the feet.

Fig. 6. Follow-up,
move in, gain and
point is to throat.

Bayonet "Gain and Point"

This is the new movement in bayonet fencing adapted by the author from the "Gain and Point" of the épée.* It will be found a highly effective bayonet movement. The initial movement is taken from the stance of *"On Guard"* by an exaggerated violent point at the opponent's lower front middle section. (Figure 5). The subsequent success of this preliminary move will be principally due to bringing, at the moment of the feint, the right foot forward directly back of the left, unnoticed by the adversary. This can be done by riveting the adversary's attention on the "low point" by the violence of this feint thrust. The right foot was concealed by the still stationary left or forward foot, and the opponent who aims to parry the low thrust will scarcely realize that he is menaced by an impending *throat* thrust (Figure 6). The latter is speedily acomplished by avoiding blade contact from the attempted parry and making an instantaneous forward lunge step of the left foot, accompanied by a gliding thrust at the throat as shown in Figure 6. The success of this movement actually depends upon the proper final execution of the gliding blade, because it is required that no final jerky indication of the throat thrust shall be given as this would immediately bring the opponent's blade up to the high parry. The entire execution of the final move, after the attacker's feint thrust has drawn but avoided the parry, if instantaneous, will find a clear road to the throat. Left arm is stiff throughout action.

*This sword movement, taught by Major William J. Herrmann, PMTC, to Mrs. Dewar was repeatedly applied by that lady in her match in New York against the women's world foil champion. Mrs. Dewar defeated the champion by repeated application of the "Gain and Point."

In and Out

This should be the slogan of every bayonet fencer, and the bayonet should be thrust and withdrawn with rapid successive movements in order that the bayonet fencer may be instantly prepared for attack or defense against other adversaries.

The Hand-cut

The chief movements prescribed for the bayonet and for the knife fencer are patterned from the sword, and are identical. In the bayonet "hand-cut" (Figure 7) and the knife "hand-cut" the attacker takes a step to the opponent's front side, then parries the opponent's blade with the edge of his own flat blade, instantly thereafter turning the sharp edge downward and cutting the opponent's front hand. The attacker follows this with a slash into the throat. The three movements preliminary to the "kill" are *"right step, left parry, hand cut."* Or, *"left step, right parry, hand cut."*

The Parry

This is executed with a powerful blade rap of the opponent's blade to right or left (Figures 8 and 9), or above or below. The parry may be made in any of these directions, but in a duel should be mixed up so as to confuse opponent. Avoid constantly parrying in same direction.

Fig. 10. Col. Biddle, right, in jab guard defense in trench.

At the Throat

This defense, as recommended with reservations, is primarily prescribed as the best guard against the bayonet in the *trench*. The rifle is held in the *"Jab Guard"* position (Figure 10) and the blade and stock of the piece, held point up perpendicularly, furnish a full length guard to confront an enemy's bayonet attack. In any event, this stance is recommended for the trench *"On Guard"* position. Firstly, because the narrow confines of the trench preclude free use of the piece in the customary *"On Guard"* position. Secondly, because the *"Jab Guard"* stance is most effective, at intimately close combat, from which to deliver a telling thrust upwards under the chin. The *"Jab Guard"* position is the safest against a bayonet attack at the throat. Present the flat blade, and parry with the edges; a more powerful parry is thus ensured. It is recommended that this guard be frequently practiced against a blunt or scabbarded bayonet. This is a comparatively easy and safe defense, even against a *series* of thrusts at the throat. It should also be borne in mind that the offensive bayonet is almost always held in the *old time* bayonet fighter's position. This renders the blade particularly easy to parry when it is thrust as a top and bottom edged blade, as shown in the picture of the old time guard position: it is much easier to parry than the flat blade as presented with sharp edge to right and recommended in this new bayonet course.

Throw Point

 In bayonet combat or duel this old fencing movement cannot be improved upon to reach an opponent too far distant for a thrust from the guard position. As shown in Figure 11, the right foot is advanced in front of the left and the point is thrown, with the blade flat above and below, sharp edge to right, into the adversary. At the same time the left arm is extended with the left hand free in the air beneath the middle of the stock, so that, when the throw is accomplished (Figure 12), the extended stock of the piece may be easily caught and the rifle restored to the necessary balance of the *"On Guard" position.*

Juggling the Piece

Commands: *"Guard"! "Short Guard"! "Jab Guard"! "Guard"!*

From the *"On Guard"* position, the rifle is quickly thrown by both hands simultaneously into the grasp of *"Short Guard"* position. The rifle is again thrown into the grasp of *"Jab Guard"* position when the right foot is brought up directly to the rear of the advanced left foot, and a slight crouch is taken. From this position the rifle is quickly thrown back into the grasp of *"On Guard,"* and the crouch is changed to the *"On Guard"* position with the right foot about sixteen inches rear.

Command: *"Pass, Shift—Parry and Point"!* The foregoing described shifts in guard are each in turn executed under a repetition of the latter command, each part of the command being executed as each particular part of the command is given. The *"pass"* here ordered is a *"front pass"* described later in "Steps" and is repeated with each shift in "guard."

Croise

An excellent method of defense and attack prescribes that a right or left parry becomes a downward parry: this by an adroit wrist turn down of one's rifle-holding front hand. This "turn down" must not be telegraphed, but applied only at contact: it should imprison the opponent's blade, then cut his hand and make way for one's "riposte" into the throat.

43

Fig. 13. Knocking down opponent is a simple matter.

The Knock Down

To knock down an opponent, parry right and instantly step in with the right foot, bringing the stock of your piece against your opponent's; then press forward against his stock and carry your left foot in the air outside and behind his forward left leg and kick violently, heel first, into the back of the calf of his left leg (Figure 13), thus making him lose his footing and fall backward. The butt stroke at the chest, as described on the first page of this chapter, should also be carried through to a "knock down."

The Defense

Colonel Miller devised the following defense: the prostrate one can avoid a death thrust from his standing adversary if he successfully encompasses with his left instep the attacker's ankle behind the heel of the latter's forward foot, and sets his own right foot firmly against the upper front shin bone of the attacker directly below the latter's knee (Figure 14).

Fig. 14. To defend self from ground, use push into leg.

Steps

Advance.—This commands a single left step and right step forward, retaining the *"On Guard"* position.

Retire.—Opposite of the *"advance"* movement, prescribing a right step and step *rear*, retaining the forward *"On Guard"* position.

Left Step.—This is most effectively made with an accompanying preliminary right parry, but in any case this is a left foot step *left*, instantly followed by bringing the right foot back of the left to *"On Guard"* position.

Right Step.—A step to the right with the right foot followed by a coordinated step to the right with the left foot to *"On Guard"* position.

Front Pass.—This commands a forward step of the right foot twelve inches to the front of advanced left foot, immediately followed by the advance of the left foot beyond the right foot to the "on guard" position.

Rear Pass.—This is a directly opposite movement to the front pass, viz., the passing of the left foot twelve inches to the rear of the right foot immediately followed by the passing of the right foot to the rear of the left foot so that the proper "guard" position is resumed.

47

Leaps

A leap is taken directly from the "guard" position with the rifle bearing bayonet *thrust* violently forward into the opponent's middle section. The spring-off of this leap can be well taken from the rear leg when it takes the second step in an *"advance."* The FRONT PASS AND LEAP is by far the best and most effective, and most terrifying to the adversary, and the leap should be taken directly following and from the forward step of the right foot.

Volts

Each "Volt" command is preceded by the words, "Right," "Left," "To the rear, right" or "To the rear, left," The *volt* is executed on the ball of the forward foot, carrying the rear foot around to conform with the *"On Guard"* position. During every *volt* the rifle barrel must be raised perpendicularly (in order to clear intervening objects) and lowered for point attack instantly on arrival in the new *"On Guard"* position (Figures 15 and 16).

Part II
KNIFE
FIGHTING

CONSIDERABLE space in this treatise is given to knife fighting because Marines serve in many knife fighting countries and are frequently called upon to capture or fight against the dagger, machete or bolo. There are countries in Asia, Europe, Central America, Africa, and South America where the knife is a chief fighting weapon. While the military police in such countries, if they be Marines as is sometimes the case, can hardly attempt to match skill in the use of the bolo, machete, dagger or other type knives of the native, they can *draw* the bayonet and apply the hand-cut which is an unknown art to the *native* knife men. The hand-cut is particularly prescribed for use with the *bayonet as knife* and is an exquisitely scientific movement, taken from the sword and known to few others than scientific swordsmen. The skilled épée fencer or duellist thrusts at the sword hand and arm of an opponent; the scienced broad-swordsman *cuts* or thrusts at the sword hand and arm. When time does not permit the attachment of the bayonet to the rifle, or when the bayonet is worn in the belt and no rifle is carried, it is prescribed to use the bayonet as a disarming weapon against the armed adversary. In fact, with a quick cut to the opponent's knife-holding hand, it is possible for the bayonet thus used to disarm several in a group of attacking knife men. There are various methods of wielding the knife in the many respective countries where the dagger is publicly and generally recognized as a standard weapon, and the overhand guard and stroke and the underhand guard and stroke are separately characteristic to particular races and are standardized and correct. Notwithstanding, the infinitely *superior* stance and method of the truly scientific knife duellist traces directly back to Roman Amphitheatre days; then the dagger duellist fought to the death. The best of these knife fighters are recorded to have been Gauls, who had been made slaves, as the gladiators were in ancient Rome. These old-time gladiators used what is still today the accepted method of the larger majority of professional or champion knife duellists. The names of the movements are Gaelic-Roman. Underhand or overhand dagger contestants confronting the cool skill of the prescribed dagger *duellist* would be at a disadvantage like the *amateur* boxer facing the professional. Hand cutting is a practically unknown art to the underhand or overhand dagger fighter, and the straight knife-hold stance of the skilled duellist places the underhand or overhand dagger fighter at a disadvantage.

But, while the Gaelic-Roman names for the knife movements are still used, the following course of instruction teaches the use of the knife as prescribed by the late Colonel James Bowie, USA. The Bowie knife has proved the most complete knife fighting method. While the colonel traced his methods of attack and defense through the lines of knife history as recited in this brief preamble, the following course of instruction is after the teachings of the Bowie knife as prescribed by the colonel himself; he was a celebrated sword duellist. The knife had its inception when Colonel Bowie broke his sword in a duel and continued his fight by closing in and killing his opponent

53

with the shortened broken blade which he still held at the hilt. Thus his newly found weapon was fashioned as a straight blade of the precise length of the broken blade with which he killed his enemy. Not only did he prove with his newly found blade to be the greatest knife fighter of his time, but it is related that when he was ill in bed he was attacked by some nine Mexican soldiers, who stole in upon him to take his life with tomahawks and knives. From his sick bed Colonel Bowie met their united attack with his Bowie knife; with this he killed seven before he himself succumbed with Colonels Travis and Crockett during the battle of the Alamo. He took a foremost part in the Texas Revolution. He opposed the Mexicans in battles during the year 1835, and eventually commanded his troops as colonel.

As is elsewhere recounted in this manual, many graduates from the U. S. Marine Corps Student Officers Basic School continue their study and practice in individual combat. They frequently return to the school and tell of subsequent experiences. An outstanding example was related at the basic school by a prominent Marine aviator. He said that he and a fellow officer had continued their individual fighting practices and that each always carries a bayonet in his belt.

In Nicaragua the two drew their bayonets against an attack of the enemy and successfully hand-cut their way to safety through this force of some twenty machete fighters. He testified that the knowledge of knife *science* saved their lives. Thus, two Marine skilled knife fighters defeated twenty machete fighting opponents.

In Germany the Army officers, the police and the Hitler Storm Troopers are now all armed with the knife which they use as either knife or bayonet.

Fig. 17. Parry to
left or outside in
preparatory move.

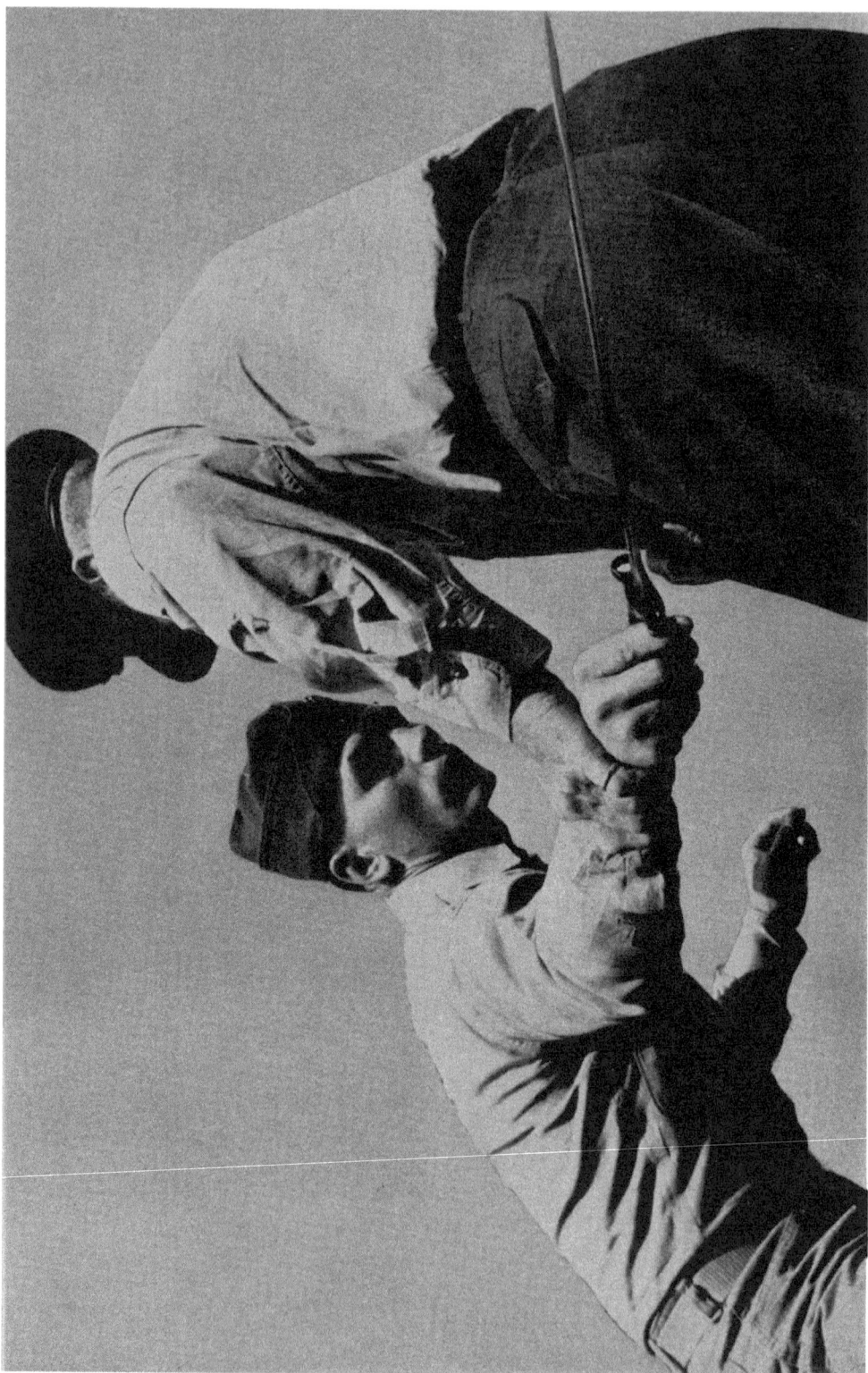

Outside Parry and Grab

To execute this movement the opponent's blade is parried toward the outside (Figure 17), and instantly afterwards the wrist of his knife hand is grasped from the outside by the disarming (left) "grab hand" of the defensive opponent who parried (Figure 18).

Inside Parry and Grab

This movement is not pictured, but is the opposite of the "outside parry and grab" as shown in the accompanying illustration. The wrist of the opponent's knife-holding hand is grasped from the inside in similar fashion immediately following a parry of his blade toward the inside—it is the opposite side "parry and grab" of the pictures here shown.

The Parry and Grab Follow-up

Wrist grabs are taken with fingers up, thumb down. And immediately following his left hand grab, the defense steps in with left foot advance.

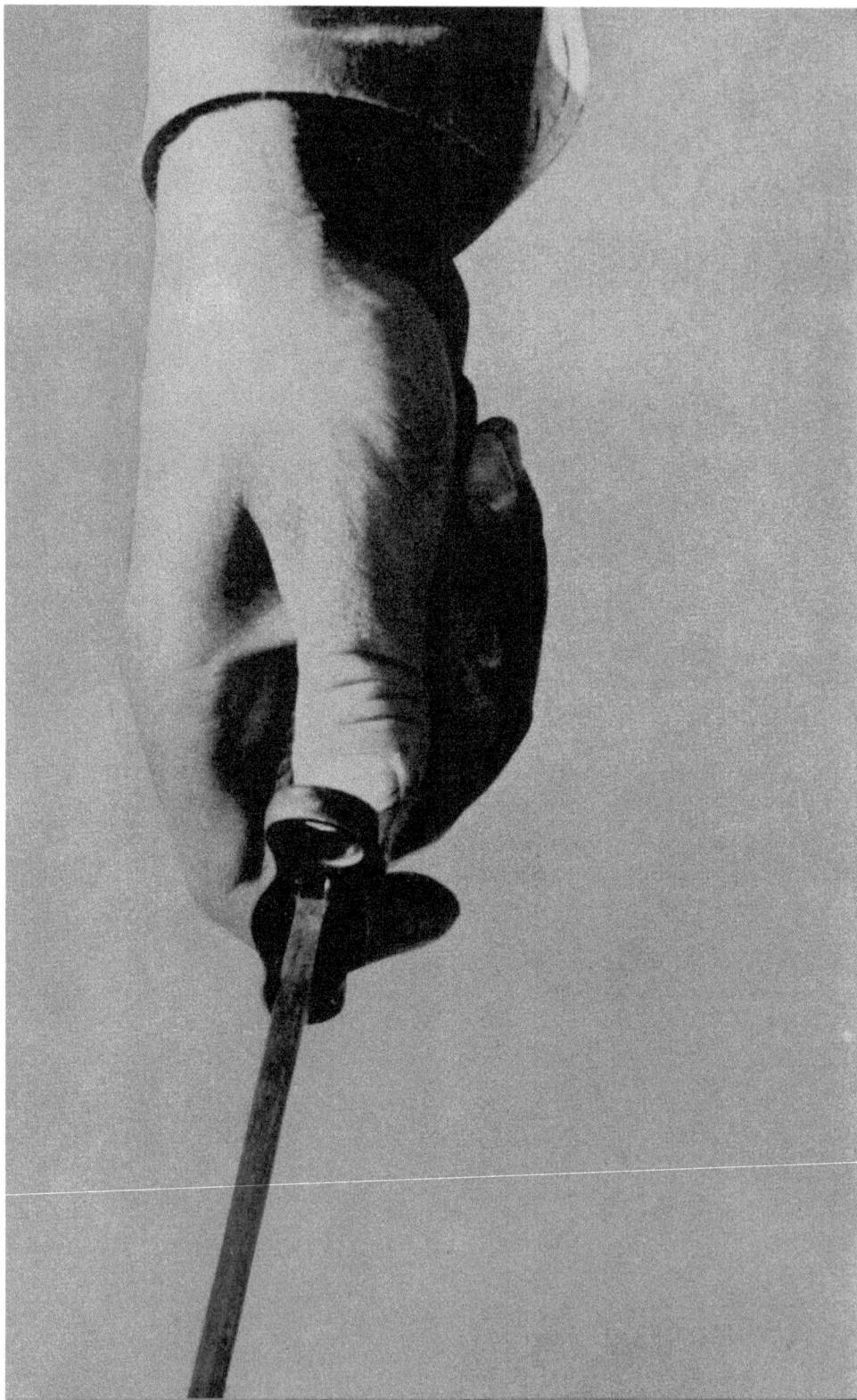

Blade Position

As prescribed in the bayonet stance, the knife is *also* held with the flat side above and below, and the cutting edge facing outward to the right (Figure 19). The knife hold is correct when, palm down, the forefinger of the knife-holding hand encircles the bayonet button at the handle. Whether held with the left hand or the right hand the blade should be held outward so that in either case the forefinger of the blade-holding hand presses against the button at the bayonet handle. The position of the blade as a detached knife or as a bayonet on the rifle is identical with the position of the blade of the French broadsword *guard* position. As the hand- or wrist-cut or thrust is the basic plan of attack in both bayonet and dagger, so it is the *basic* attack of the épée swordsman, and it is also a particularly effective attack of the broadswordsman. In point of fact, it is the particularly scientific attack known to best *swordsmen* and rarely known to bayonet fighters or knife men. The ordinary bayonet fighting course does not teach the hand-cut, and the usual stab and slash dagger man knows nothing of this scientific play. The natural skill and celerity of the bolo or machete in native hands is definitely offset by the hand-cut which is a swordsman's science.

On Guard

Command: *"On Guard"!*

The correct guard position of the dagger is shown in Figure 17, at start of a parry. It will be seen that the left hand is ever ready to apply the grab as shown in Figure 18. This picture represents the start of what is known as "Outside Parry and Grab."

Extend Left Arm Rear in Right Thrusts

Always follow the swordsman's method of throwing out your left arm straight rear when making a right hand thrust; it adds velocity and balance. See *Stoccata*, Figure 20.

In-quartata

Command: *"In-quartata—Time—Thrust"!*

To accomplish the In-quartata thrust, step with the left foot to the rear and right of the right foot as shown in the foot position of Figure 21. But in the *precise* in-quartata movement the left step right rear is accompanied by a *quarte* thrust at the lower body of the opponent which the changed thrust position has placed unguarded, "out of line."

The opposite of the in-quartata movement is called Stoccata and consists of a left step to left and thrust to lower right body as shown in Figure 20.

Fig. 21. In-quartata
thrust follows the
feinting movement.

Passata Sotto

Command: *"Passata Sotto—Time—Thrust"!*

This movement is executed on an opponent who lunges forward with a high thrust. It is so graphically illustrated in Figure 22 that a detailed description seems unnecessary. Here the more skilled knife fighter avoids the thrust of an adversary by stooping to his own left under his adversary's outstretched arm and bringing the dagger point to the middle section of his adversary

Unarmed Defense Against Overhand Dagger Assault

The accompanying illustrations show how the unarmed man may successfully defend himself against the overhand dagger thrust. This particular defense is prescribed by Major William J. Herrmann, PMTC, former World's Bayonet Fighting Champion. The faster and more violent the attack, the easier this defense is of accomplishment. A quick upward jolt with the left hand at the elbow of the attacking arm completely deflects and throws aside the attacker (Figures 23 and 24).

The writer especially recommends the favorite unarmed defense which the late Colonel Miller prescribed against the overhand dagger assault. The following is Colonel Miller's own celebrated instruction in this movement: "Catch the blow of the opponent's descending right forearm on your left bent forearm, step in quickly and pass your right arm in rear of the opponent's right upper arm (knife arm), so that your right hand or fist rests in front of the opponent's right forearm just above the elbow— then bend the opponent backwards, breaking the arm."

66

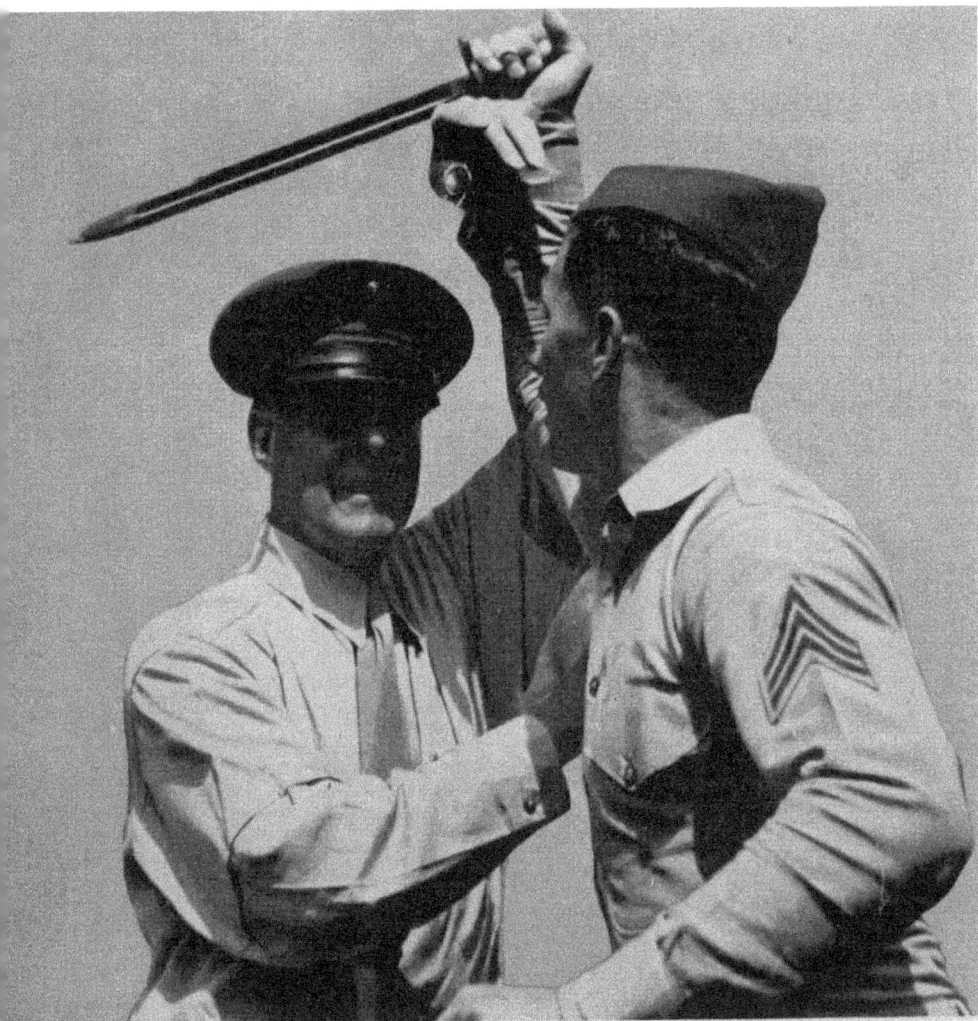

Fig. 23. Unarmed
man stops thrust
with left forearm.

The Chair Sword Contest

The sword is the master weapon of all the blades. A complete defense can be had by skillful wrist movements of the seated sword scientist; he must score his point with the riposte.

At the Cercle Hoche in Paris, where the author frequently fenced with men many years older than himself, he recalls the special skill of a Monsieur Priam, an elderly gentleman more than seventy-two years of age who, at the time, continued to be one of the great foil professionals of France. In his fencing bouts he scarcely ever found it necessary to take a single step, for he could hold an adversary at bay with exquisite sword play from his scientific wrist, and he scored his point with a "riposte" from his parry of the opponent's lunge.

Part III
JIU-JITSU
and SAVATE

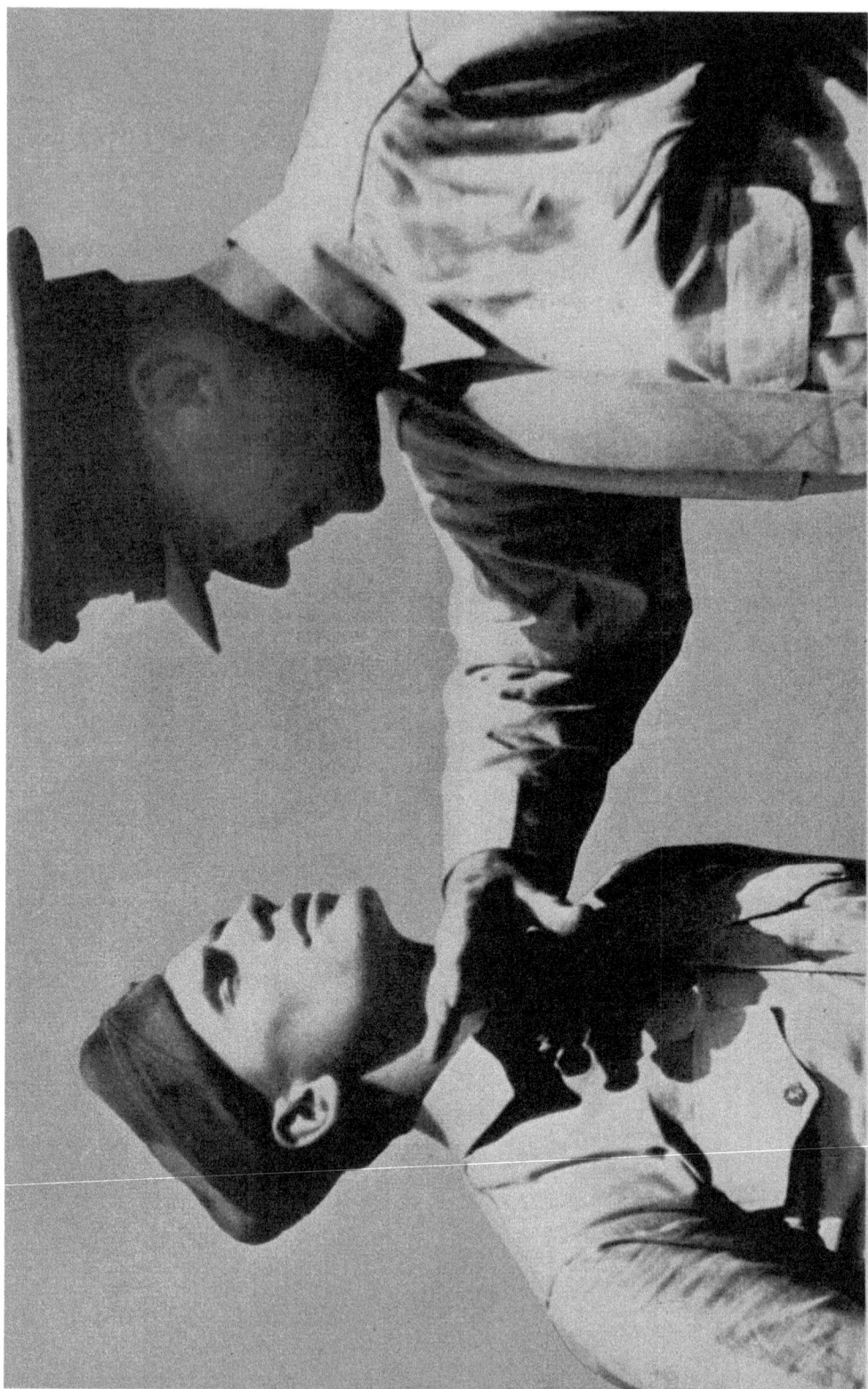

T HE selection of the very few Jiu-Jitsu movements prescribed in this course is particularly made along the lines of least effort, and the movements are such that require little or no strength, but only quickness of thought and action. In fact, they are all Jiu-Jitsu movements such as a quick-thinking, able-bodied woman can readily be taught to use. For instance, when one is attacked by a double-handed grasp on one's throat, the intended victim's own hands should be immediately clasped and brought violently up together between the extended arms of the throttler. This will instantly disengage the throttler's grasp and throw his arms out of line; then the defense cups his hands and simultaneously claps the ears of his assailant. Such a counter-attack will likely break the ear drums of the marauder. Another defense is to seize a finger of the throttler and break it.

All Jiu-Jitsu wrestling movements that require particular science in trying for complicated holds or grasps are avoided. The Jiu-Jitsu movements herein shown are strongly advocated for use at close quarters either when weaponless and confronting an armed opponent or when holding a weapon in one's own

*Jiu-Jitsu—Japanese, JuJutsu: freely translated, skill or dexterity (Jutsu) employed without fighting instruments (Ju).

73

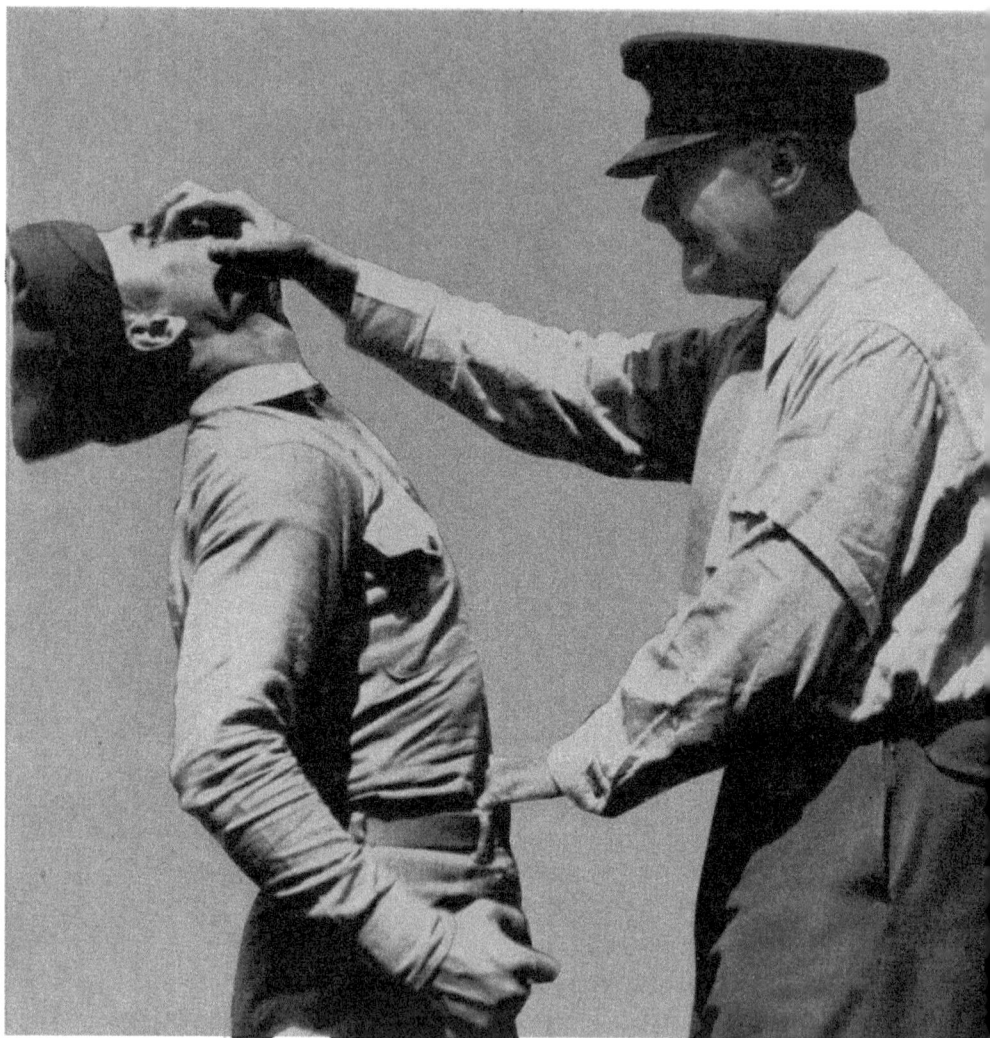

Fig. 26. To make
eyes out attack,
use entire hand.

hands. Two particularly effective Jiu-Jitsu movements are shown in the pictures on "breaking the windpipe" (Figure 25), and "Eyes Out" (Figure 27).

The point of the drive should come entirely from the forward thrust from the biceps and shoulder. The delivery of the blow in this way is required to make it successful. The fingers and wrist must be rigid. Delivering the throat attack, as prescribed in Figure 25, will sever the windpipe; and in the "Eyes Out" assault, illustrated in Figure 27, the first and second fingers are passed into and through the eyes.

The defense against "Eyes Out" prescribes one's own wide open hand held perpendicularly, outer edge forward, thumb in and against the nose between the eyes.

Defendu and Jiu-Jitsu

Lieutenant Colonel Samuel G. Taxis, whose initial lessons in Jiu-Jitsu were taught him by the writer, brought to the Marine Corps the science of the celebrated Mr. W. E. Fairbairn, originator of "Defendu." Colonel Taxis has instructed a battalion of the Fourth Regiment of Marines in Jiu-Jitsu and Defendu. This the colonel did in China where he trained and managed the Marine boxing team that won the boxing championship of China.

Colonel Taxis also took part as an instructor with Mr. Fairbairn, in teaching Jiu-Jitsu and Defendu to 200 Sikh police. There were few defenses against Jiu-Jitsu attacks before Mr. Fairbairn entered the field, but Colonel Taxis now shows a perfect defense against every one of the innumerable Jiu-Jitsu "holds" and "blows."

In the "Eyes Out" attack, the movement of Colonel Taxis requires less accuracy than is needed to execute the attack in

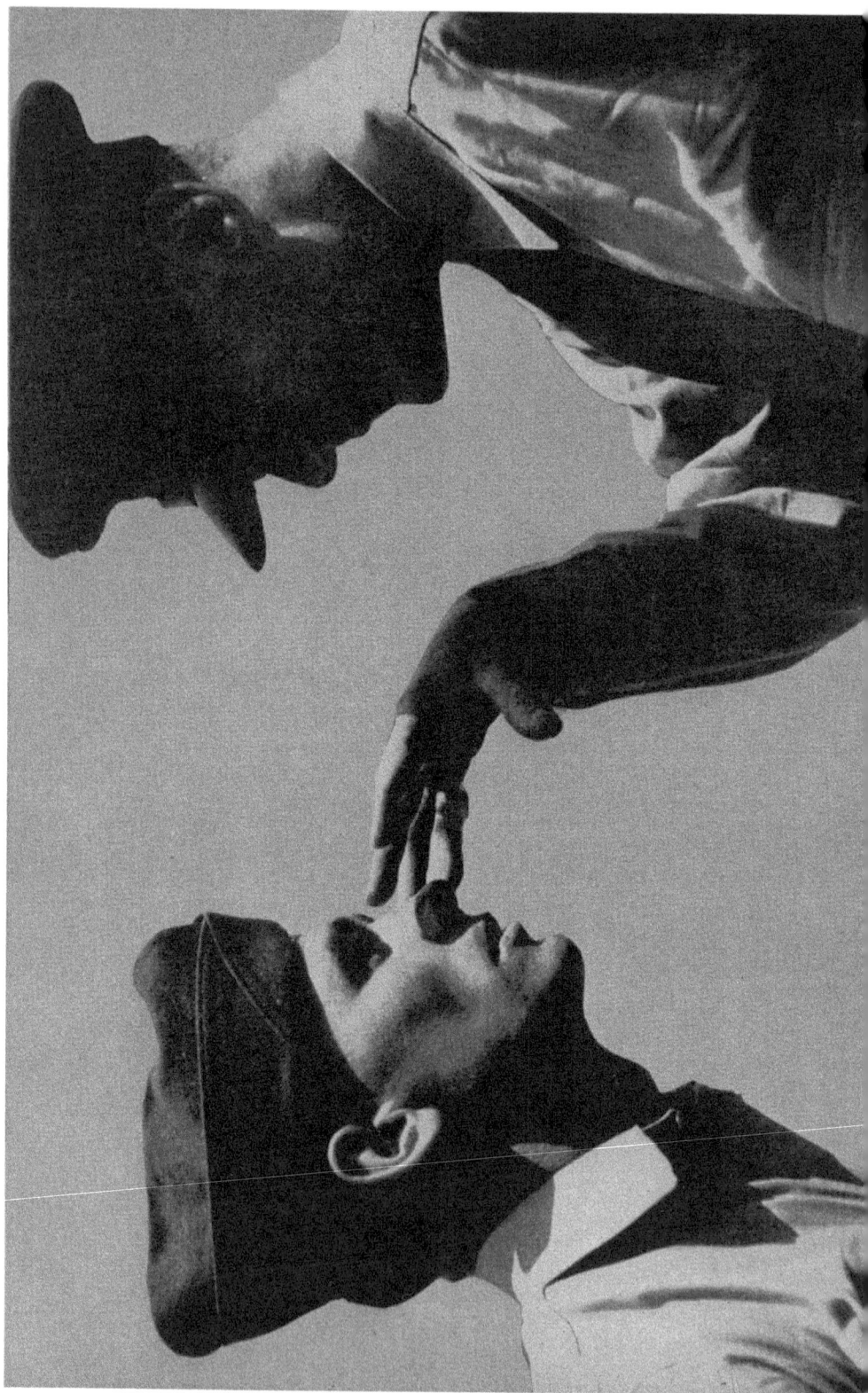

Figure 27. (The heel of either right or left hand is placed against the opponent's chin, and the fingers are pressed or scratched into the opponent's eyes.) This movement can be most adroitly accomplished by applying it to the upper hand in the Colonel Miller attack (see Figure 26).

Colonel Taxis delivers all his Defendu and Jiu-Jitsu blows from the outer edge of the wide open stiffened hand, which he uses like a weapon.

He prefers this attack at the throat instead of the straightened finger attack as shown in "Break the Windpipe" (Figure 25).

By striking a person with the outer edge of the hand a smart blow in front, directly below the ribs, the solar plexus is reached (Figure 28); a similar smart blow from above between the neck and shoulder can break the collar bone (Figure 29); the *vital* blow is delivered at the point over the thinnest bone where the nose joins the head between the eyes (Figure 30). The bone here is as thin as paper, and a blow downward directly breaking this bone causes a brain hemorrhage which brings blood poison in the brain and death within sixteen to twenty hours.

Lieut. Col. William A. Kengla, who was a former pupil of the author in individual combat, has become an expert in Jiu-Jitsu. He has shown genius in the application of Jiu-Jitsu movements; and, along the line of Jiu-Jitsu, he has developed several movements. Figures show graphically the manner in which an unruly person can be effectively handled. The man who would take another man captive catches, with his own right hand, fingers up and thumb down, the other's *left* hand fingers from behind, and brings the hand forward so that the now

Fig. 29. Hard blow at neck can break enemy's collar bone.

unruly's arm is bent at right angles. He grasps the biceps above the elbow with his left hand and brings the unruly's bended elbow-joint directly into and against the receptacle of his own bent right arm. Retaining his grasp of the outstretched fingers, he can then completely control the further movements of a captive or lead him to a place of detention by bending the captive's wrist inward with his capture finger hold. (See Figure 31.)

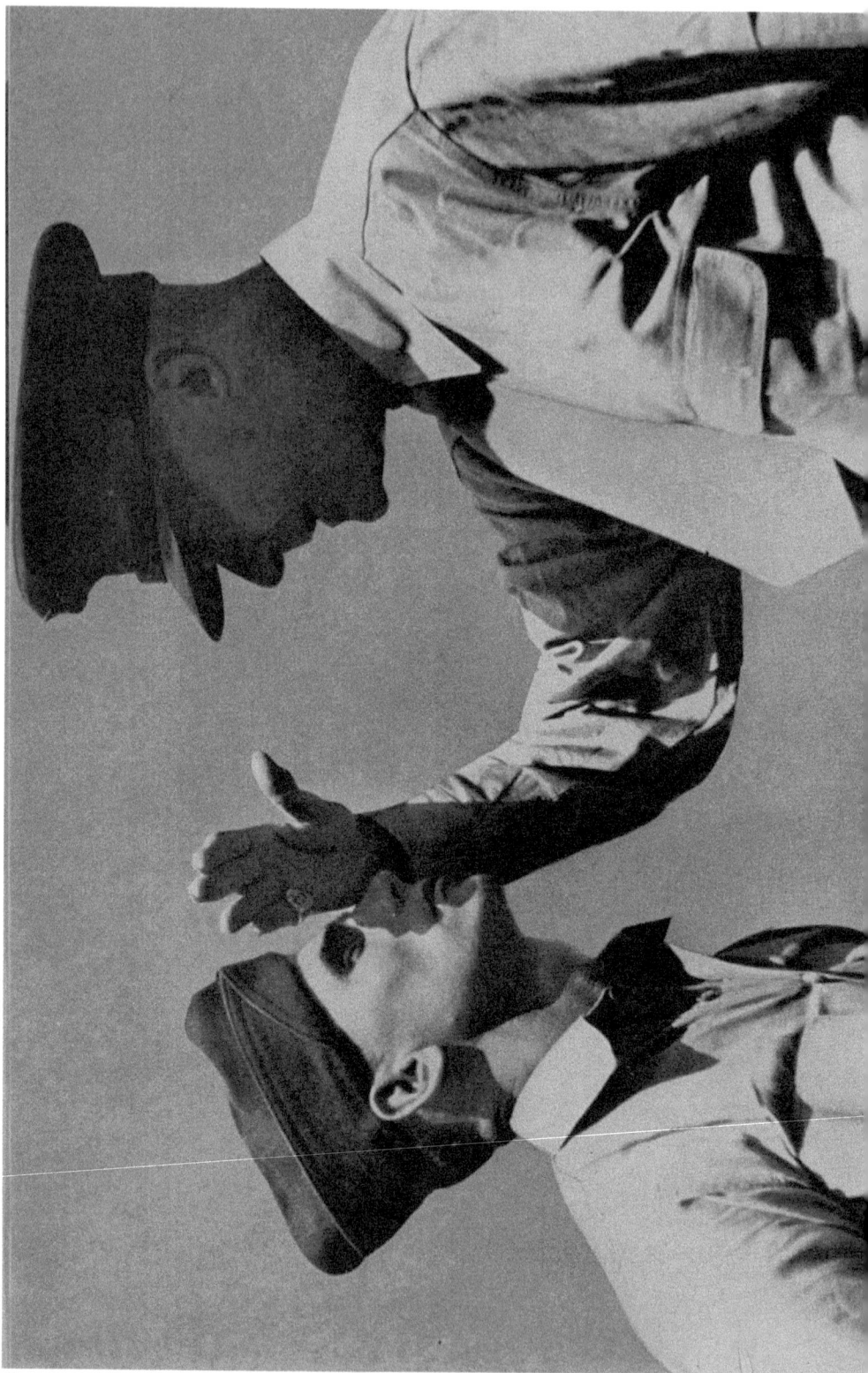

Fig. 31. A finger
hold will tame an
unruly opponent.

Pistol Disarming from the Rear

Situation.—You are caught by an opponent behind you, with the barrel of his pistol in your back. Your hands are up at his command, "Hands up, or I'll shoot"! or "Move, and I'll shoot"!

Action.—Keep the elbows closely touching the sides of the body and elevate the hands. Under no circumstances let the elbows leave the body or elevate the hands higher than in the illustration of "Pistol Disarming from the Front" (Figure 32). Turn quickly to the left, hitting the opponent's wrist with the left elbow. This must not be in any manner a push, but must be an actual blow of the elbow. Make this blow a distinct movement, instantly following it by a left arm revolution of the opponent's right arm. The revolution of the arm will reverse the elbow-joint so that good pressure will break the arm and, in the strain suffered by the opponent, his pistol can be easily taken by the right hand of the defense.

Pistol Disarming from the Front

When the assailant presses the muzzle of his pistol in front against his intended victim's middle and says, "Hands up, or I'll shoot"! the intended victim is strictly cautioned to elevate his arms precisely as shown in Figure 32, and *no higher*, elbows pressed against sides. In spite of the enemy's further warning, "Move and I'll shoot"! the intended victim is then advised to whip his left hand down, fingers up and thumb down, to a tight grasp of the enemy's pistol-hand wrist (Figure 33), and sweep the hand along to his own right in order to deflect the shot of the attacker. Many tests of this move have proven it to be completely effective. The enemy will invariably pull the trigger, and is rarely successful in shooting the victim. Figure 34 shows

Fig. 32. Start of pistol disarming from the front.

Fig. 33. Deflecting
path of bullet is
the second phase.

Fig. 34. Disarm an
adversary with a
blow at the wrist.

the intended victim about to smash at hand and disarm the marauder. A better follow-up movement, which is directly prescribed in Jiu-Jitsu is, with left grasp still on wrist, to take an instant grasp with one's right hand on the opponent's pistol-holding hand. Take the grasp with the forefinger placed directly on top of the assailant's trigger finger. By bending the pistol-holding hand inward at the wrist, and suddenly pressing the trigger finger of the enemy, he is made to shoot himself. Figure 35, of this *front* pistol disarming series presents this excellent follow-up movement, devised by Lieutenant Colonel Kengla; in addition the knee may be brought instantly up, Jiu-Jitsu fashion, into the crotch of the adversary.

An excellent rebuttal to the Jiu-Jitsu disarmament of the pistol onslaught is furnished by Maj. Gen. Julian C. Smith, United States Marines. He suggests:

In holding up a man with a pistol, keep at least three paces distance from him. If this is not possible, and the pistol must be held within his reach, instead of attempting to pull the trigger at his first movement, draw the right (pistol) hand smartly to the rear, avoiding the sweep of the opponent's left hand, and step back quickly with the right foot; bring the right forearm to a horizontal position with the wrist against the right side, keep the pistol pointed at the assailant (continuing the backward movement if necessary) and pull the trigger. At this close range the so-called "hip shot," which is really a waist shot, should be effective. The left hand is free to guard against the right hand punch to the jaw. Even if the pistol hand is grasped, the backward movement will tend to keep the pistol pointed at the opponent so the shot cannot be evaded; it also defeats the knee into the crotch movement.

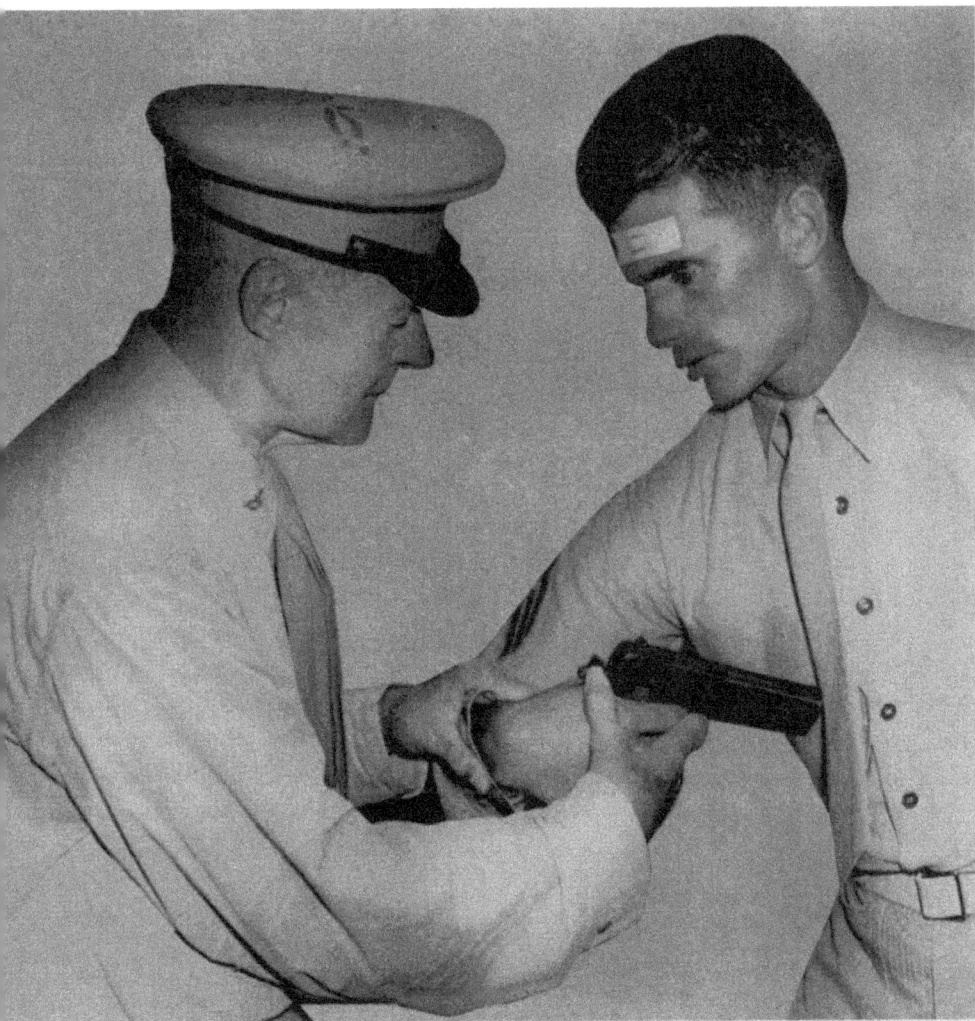

Fig. 35. You can
make enemy shoot
himself like this.

Arm Break

Of the almost innumerable effective movements in Jiu-Jitsu and Defendu, none other can surpass in immediate effectiveness the arm breaking movement. Left hand palm downwards grasp with inner left thumb knuckle, pressing, between opponent's right hand outside second and third finger hand knuckles, and with one's second finger grasped around and pressing inside of opponent's thumb. With this grasp, his forearm must be brought into a position directly at right angles with his upper arm. Now by applying pressure the opponent's wrist must be bent inwardly at an outside angle to opponent's forearm. With one's left hand second finger and thumb applied in positions as prescribed, the opponent's right hand wrist and arm at the elbow-joint will be broken unless he is quick enough to prevent the break by falling to his right instantly to the ground.

Fig. 36. Breaking an
arm is one of best
Jiu-Jitsu movements.

Gentle Grasps

Be certain to always take *gentle* grasps with your left hand and distract the opponent's attention by right hand gestures until you have brought the opponent's right hand into position for the final twist: then put instant pressure into your execution.

Hand Shakes

To subjugate a man with the hand shake and with the deception necessary in Jiu-Jitsu, take an especially tight grasp of his right hand and elevate it and slip the left hand underneath his right arm to a grasp on the top of his left shoulder (Figure 36). Straighten your left arm so that it comes directly below your opponent's right elbow, and be careful to hold his palm up. Thus, by exerting pressure downwards in your grasp of your opponent's right hand you can readily break his arm at his elbow.

Or, by retaining your tightened grasp you can subjugate your opponent by quickly stooping and passing your head either to the right or to the left under the hand clasp. In either position to which you then arrive by straightening up, with your still retained hand clasp you have your opponent in an imprisoned position through the twists of his arm which have been brought about through your own movements.

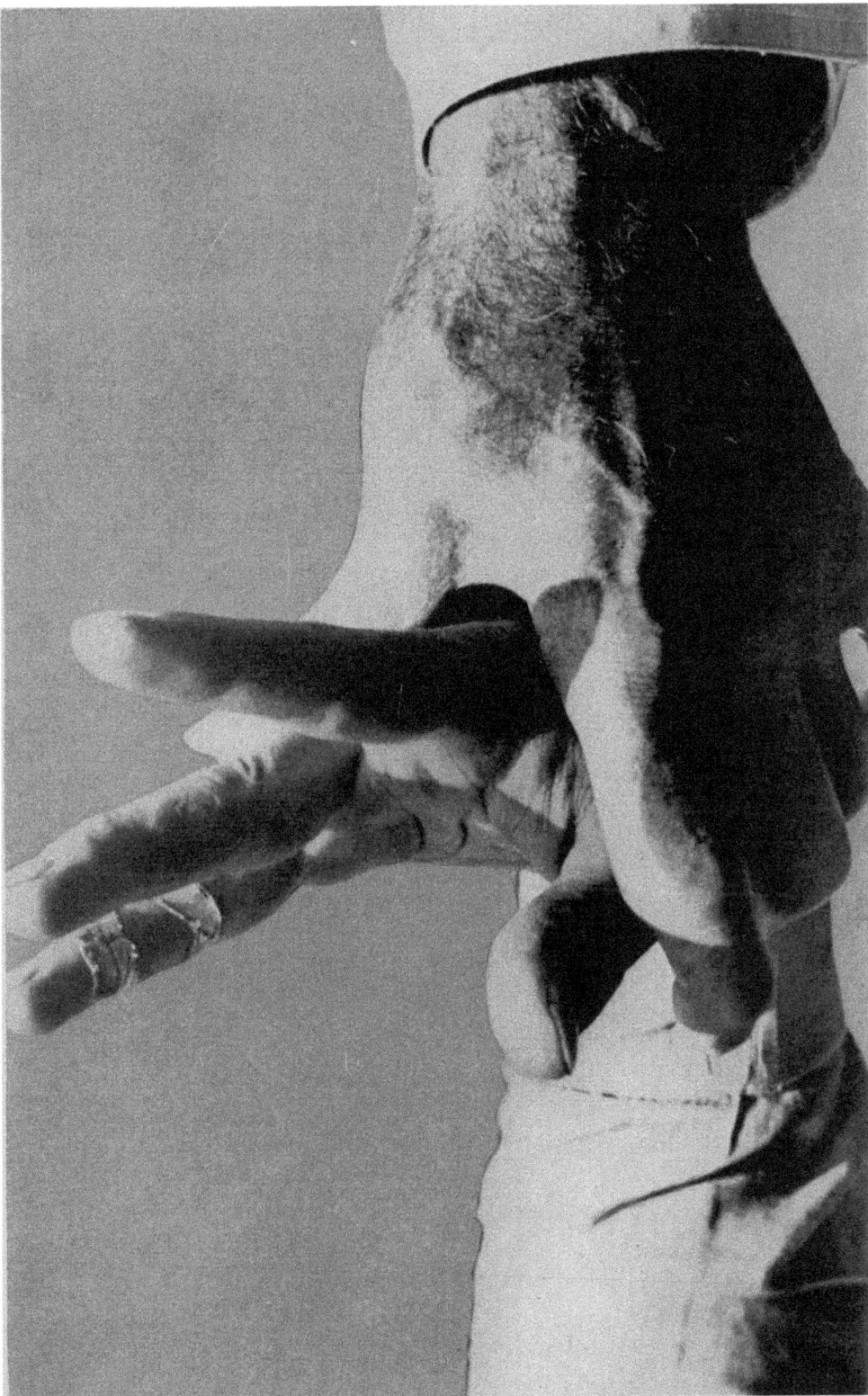

Defense Against a Hand Push

If a man places the palm of his hand against you to push you backwards, place either or both of your hands against his hand and hold it and bend forward. Thus you can break his wrist (Figure 37).

The Finger Subjugation

When an opponent has grasped you around the middle to bend you backwards with his hands clasped behind you, straighten your forefinger and second finger and press them on his upper or lower lip. Here the nerve-centres around the lower and upper gums of the teeth are super-sensitive, and direct finger pressure will cause the strongest man to drop his hold. But all such finger pressure must be executed with the fingers straightened parallel with one's hand and arm. Pressure from bent fingers from a bent wrist is not effective.

To Lead a Person at Will

With your left hand grasp the first three fingers of another's right hand, thumb inside of his fingers and lift his hand with his palm upwards with pressure downwards in your grasp on his fingers (Figure 38). He will submit to your authority.

Arm Thrust and Belt Hold

This is one of the best movements for disarming or taking prisoner, and it is comparatively easy of accomplishment. In the Arm Thrust or Belt Hold the assailant or unruly offender is grasped quickly with the left hand under the front of the belt or the upper front of the trousers, while the heel of the right hand at the same time is instantly pressed upwards against the opponent's chin (see Figure 26).

Savate

Following a life's study of various standardized systems of Individual Combat among the world's peoples, certain movements appear noteworthy. Frenchmen fight with their feet in *Savate:* the toe kick is "taboo," and blow delivery is from the sole of the foot. One such blow is herein prescribed (Figure 39); it is aimed at the front shin bone directly below the adversary's knee. It breaks the knee-joint. Such a blow is recommended in a fist fight when the assault drives one backward: then duck down, bending backward to the right and deliver the sole of the forward left foot as a blow.

If threatened or attacked when seated, this identical foot-blow with right or left foot on the standing adversary is instantly followed by a right or left "hook" punch to his open jaw: his mouth invariably opens as the man careens forward with invective surprise or renewed attack. The open jaw is easily broken. Several other *Savate* attacks are prescribed with Jiu-Jitsu in this manual.

95

Knee in the Crotch or Break the Instep

This is *Jiu-Jitsu* or *Defendu*. When the assailant imprisons one's hands and arms, lift the knee violently into his crotch (Figure 40) or, again, stamp on his instep; a heavy stamp will break the instep.

Frisking

This is another effective "foreign" assault. Straighten and stiffen the fingers and scrape their tips rapidly back and forth across the eyes and nose bridge of your intended victim. (Also see Jiu-Jitsu attack, "Eyes Out," Figure 27.)

Remember!

You are *never* defenseless. The assailant's eyes are an easy mark. At close range a handful of gravel or any handy article might be thrown at the eyes, or a hat whipped into them.

Lt. Col. Taxis prescribes that a handkerchief worn in the upper left-hand coat pocket can be loaded with a few buckshot sewed, in small bulk, into one corner. Such handkerchief can be seized out at the top edge by the right hand, and the loaded corner can be deftly flicked into the eyes of an assailant.

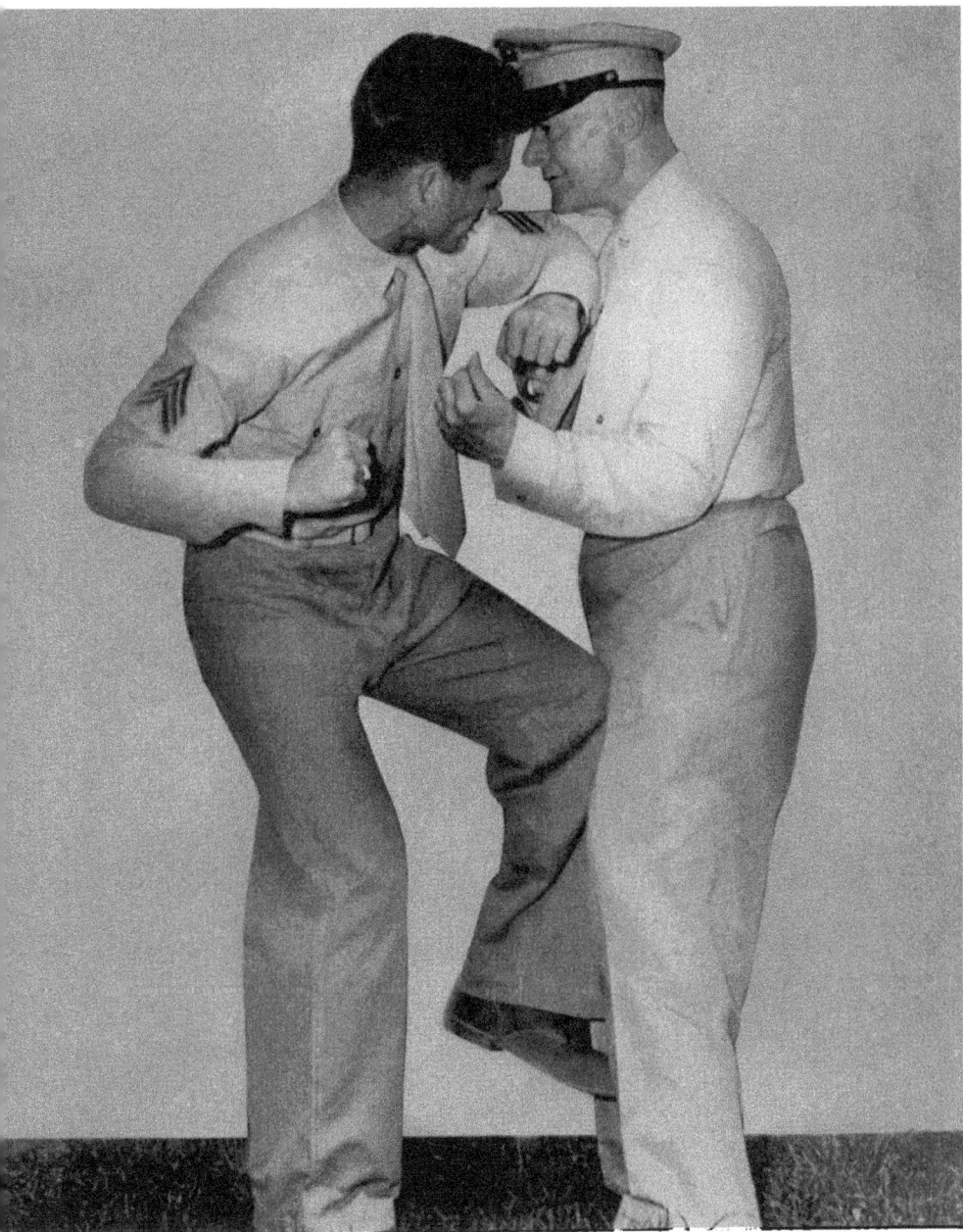

Fig. 40. Lift knee
into crotch with
force to disable.

Part IV
BOXING

THE only death-dealing play devised in boxing was invented by the late Robert Fitzsimmons, who, until Gene Tunney, was perhaps the greatest genius in ring history. Tunney was at all times merciful. Although himself a middleweight, Fitzsimmons held three world championships, being middleweight, light-heavyweight, and heavyweight champion.

As the writer was privileged to be one of the sparring partners of Fitzsimmons, that mighty fighter took especial pains to carefully instruct the writer in the intricacies of the boxing movements of his own invention. These were supremely remarkable but, strangely enough, the knowledge of them has not generally been carried down to posterity.

He developed one punch which was sure to kill if landed with killing intent, but, with such dangerous knowledge, Fitzsimmons had an unusually kind and sympathetic nature which forbade undue cruelty. In an encounter he was long-suffering to a fault. In spite of this, few fighters withstood the Fitzsimmons punch, and he fought, in all, 328 battles, of which he lost but five, two of these being to the same man, the great James J. Jeffries.

Fig. 41. Start of a knockout punch is a right hook to chin.

The Killing Shift

This was the movement with which Fitzsimmons scored his knockouts. With the shift he won the heavyweight championship of the world over the late James J. Corbett. To execute the shift, a right hook is aimed at the opponent's chin; at the same time the right foot steps forward, adding speed and force to the blow. This right step must land toes forward with the heel or back of the foot securely placed directly against and in rear of the opponent's forward left foot (Figure 41). Then, if the onslaught of the right hook fails to land, the assailant's body continues to follow the course of his hook that missed (Figure 41). Here he must let the momentum of his own unlanded right hooked punch carry him down to the left until his left crooked forearm is at right angles on the outside directly below his own left knee (Figure 42). Then he straightens up his right arm, which he swings quickly as a pivot to speed a left hand punch which travels from below the outside of his slightly bended left knee to the underpoint of the opponent's chin (Figure 43). As he hurls this punch, he puts the entire weight of his body back of it by straightening both knees which he had bent to add the weight of his body to the blow. While chin punches from a standing position may break the jaw, the punch from underneath, if delivered correctly and with full force, will drive the upper jaw bones into the base of the brain and thereby cause brain concussion which can result in death to the victim. But Fitzsimmons used a preliminary blow to pave the way for his "knockout" just described: it places the opponent "off guard"

Fig. 42. If right fails to land, go into this position.

and precisely posed to receive the "finishing punch." To accomplish this, execute the shift into the final position preceding the left hand jaw punch. Then, instead of punching the jaw, straighten up with a drive of one's left fist into the solar plexus (Figure 44). This region can be reached by a punch-push into the opponent's front middle section directly below the ribs above the stomach. By driving the blow in deep to the solar plexus, the opponent is momentarily paralyzed: he will sag at the knees, drop his hands and droop, chin forward, into the exact position to receive the jaw "knockout." And now, be sure and go all the way back to the stooping posture, as first described, for delivery of the final punch to the jaw; ample time will be had if the solar plexus was reached, for thus the opponent is rendered temporarily helpless.

The late Stanley Ketchell told the writer that he had carefully copied the Fitzsimmons shifts in his own onslaughts, which he himself so brilliantly executed, but even Ketchell never obtained the knowledge of the combination which is herein disclosed. Ketchell gained his masterful hitting power by shifting the foot with each punch, but he did not carry his shifts through as herein described because of his incomplete knowledge of the Fitzsimmons method.

The writer most carefully instructed that celebrated athlete, Lieutenant Colonel Alan Shapley, USMC, of an All-American football team, in the art of the Fitzsimmons shift. Col. Shapley became more adept in this particular style of boxing than anyone the writer has ever seen, since Fitzsimmons. He has scored

Fig. 43. The telling
punch comes up to
the chin from floor.

many knockouts as a boxer, and uses the Fitzsimmons shift to perfection.

The Fitzsimmons side-step is the best, but it also is unknown among the boxers today. It furnishes the easiest and surest avoidance of the peerless *left jab*. On the instant of an opponent's left lead, his adversary pivots, heel left, on the ball of his forward left foot so that his toes face directly to the right. At the same moment, he lifts his right foot an inch from the ground and replaces it. The logic *that we think with the feet* is thus proven true, as no other movement is required to remove oneself out of harm's way from the left jab. Ducking or parrying are both too slow. The Fitzsimmons side-step, once thoroughly mastered, is the surest and safest method of avoiding the most devastating of all boxing attacks—the *left jab*. This left jab was the favorite attack of the late James J. Corbett, as it has since been of almost all the world's most *expert* boxers. It won the championship for Gene Tunney against Jack Dempsey.

Fig. 44. Optional preliminary punch is to solar plexus.

The Neck Grab, Rabbit Punch and Pivot Blow

The third invention of Fitzsimmons is especially recommended for individual combat. Feint a blow with either hand at the opponent's face, and, instead of hitting, open the hand and grasp him at the back of the neck. Immediately pull him quickly forward so that his head is down. In his staggering position, slap him on the back of the neck alternately with the open palm of each hand until he becomes groggy. Then, as you let his head up, a smash with the fist will "do the trick." The outlawed pivot blow is excellent in rough and tumble fighting. Directly following a frontal attack, the combatant pivots right in a complete circle, on the ball of his rear right foot and, with a bended right arm, strikes his victim's face with the outside of his crooked upper right elbow (Figure 45).

END

Fig. 45. Following a pivot, elbow is used to hit face.

www.ingramcontent.com/pod-product-compliance
Lightning Source LLC
Chambersburg PA
CBHW051218150426

42812CB00053BA/2501